SUCCESSFUL SELF

(Successful Tools for Residential Non-Governmental Transitional Housing)

(STRNGTH)

A 36 Week Curriculum based on the 8 Step Eco Map for at risk, incarcerated, and reentry.

By Gene R. Hill, Sr. & Brenda Hill

SUCCESSFUL SELF
Successful Tools for Residential Non-Governmental Transitional Housing
(STRNGTH)

A 36 Week Curriculum based on the 8 Step Eco Map for at risk, incarcerated, and reentry.
By Gene R. Hill, Sr. & Brenda Hill
©2015

Print ISBN#: 978-0-9969009-0-4
Digital Book ISBN#: 978-0-9969009-1-1

Publisher: TEAM PUBLICATIONS, LLC
4310 Ryan St; Suite 134
Lake Charles, LA 70605
337-474-2210

In conjunction with
Gene R. Hill, Sr. & Brenda Hill
Successful Self, Inc.
4219 Worthy Drive
Lake Charles, LA 70607

Unless otherwise noted, all scripture is taken from various Bible publications (ie: KJV, NKJV, etc) and fall under the "Gratis Use" guidelines.

"Scripture quotations taken from the Amplified® Bible, Copyright © 1954, 1958, 1962, 1964, 1965, 1987 by The Lockman Foundation Used by permission." (www.Lockman.org)

8 Step Eco Map designed by Levert Blount III
© Gene R. Hill, Sr. and Brenda Hill

Cover and Illustrations by Jordain Cross
© Gene R. Hill, Sr. and Brenda Hill

All Rights Reserved. No part of this publication may be reproduced, stored in a retrieval system or transmitted in any form or by any means–electronic, mechanical, digital, photocopy, recording, or any other–except for brief quotations in printed reviews, without the prior permission of the authors and/or publisher.

Table of Contents

Non-Essential Questions / Word Study..4
Words About Life..5
Words That Turn on a Light...6
The Gospel Enacted..8
Successful Self (STRNGTH)...9
STRNGTH Phase I & II..10
The Gospel Re-Enacted..11
Unit I: Breath of Life / Spiritual..12
Unit II: This is How I Learn / Education....................................15
Unit III: Where is my Father / Family..18
Unit IV: I Was Called / Career..21
Unit V: Eye Witness / Legal...24
Unit VI: Fit for the Kingdom / Health: Medical & Mental.......27
Unit VII: A Full House / Estate...30
Unit VIII: A Helpful Tool / Finance..33
CELEBRATION!!...36
Conclusion...39
Fatherhood Statistics..40
About the Authors..41

Non-Essential Questions

1. Who is God?

2 What is Spirit?

3. Who is the Holy Ghost?

4. What is Carnal?

5: What is Soul?

6. What does God desire of man?

Word Study

Justified - make right or declare as one ought to be

Faith – steadfast confident trust in God or Jesus the Christ

Peace – rest, safety, security, tranquility, completeness

Access – to lead unto, a moving to, approach

Rejoice – to cry aloud, be merry or delighted, exult

Hope – expectation, the thing I long for

Glory – beauty, purity, grace, magnificence

Patience – bear long, suffer long, endure, slow to avenge

Tribulation – affliction, to trouble or press hard upon, distress

Experience – trial, proof, testing, observe diligently

Words About Life

Love... to have in bosom, pity, or to be merciful
  (Agape...all in reference to God)
  (Phileo...brotherly kindness)
  (Thelo...to will, to wish, to desire, or to intent)
  (Eros or Erotic...pertaining to sexual desire and/or stimulations, romance)

Instructions... cause to act wisely, discipline in education, sharpen, chastisement and self-control

Fellowship... joint partakers with, communion, citizenship, and heirs together, intimacy

Eternal life... perpetual, everlasting, never to cease, to last forever

Commitment... responsibility, accountability, pledge, promise and agreement

Mediator... umpire, arbitrator, referee, intervene, negotiate

Submit... surrender to authority, obey and be subject to

Success... be wise, circumspect and prosper, prudent, triumphant, favorable

Absolute... perfect, entire, actual and complete, supreme

Depression... hopelessness, dis-heartened and saddened, unfulfilled desire

Anxiety... trouble in mind, uncertain fears, uneasy, distress

Dejection... to lower the spirit, downcast or discouraged

Fear... horror, terror, panic, dread, anxiety

Words That Turn on a Light

Spirit
Breath of God; Wind; God's Will;
Third Person in the Trinity
I Co 2:9-16

Mind
Imagination; Heart; Soul,
Thought; Spirit; Intellect
I Co. 2:16, Eph. 4:17, 23
Col. 2:18, I Tim 6:5, II Tim 3:8

Blind
Closed and Hardened, To Veil;
Covering
John 12:40

Heart
Breath; Soul; Bowels
Inner Man; Understanding
Mat. 12:35-45, 13:15

Soul
Living Being, Will, Liberty
Mat. 10:28

Light
Brightness, Illumination; Enlightenment
Mat. 5:14, 16; John. 1:9; II Co. 4:4, 6

Diligence
Accuracy, Exactness, Earnest Investigation
Heb. 11:6; II Pet. 1:5

Liberty
Free flowing; Released from Bondage/Imprisonment,
Authority; Remission of Sins
Lk: 4:18; I Co. 8:9

Darkened
Hide or Grow Dim; Conceal;
To be Consumed; Be Black
Eph. 4:18; Rm 1:21 & 11:10

Seek
Require; Enquire; Investigate;
Question; Desire; To Call; To Pray
Aim At; Search For; Demand
Mat. 6:33; Ro. 10:17; Heb. 11:6

Gospel
Goodness; To Tell Good News Before Hand;
Goodwill
I Co. 1:17, 15:1-5; Lk. 7:22

Forever
Hidden Time; Duration; Today, Yesterday, Tomorrow
Gen. 43:9; Deut. 4:40

The Gospel Enacted

INTRODUCTION

*In the beginning was Information (**Word**). Information (**Word**) was with God. Information (**Word**) was God. Not one thing came into being without Information (**Word**). Information (**Word**) was made flesh and blood and dwelt among us.* (John 1:1, 14 paraphrased, italics mine).

The Gospel really is 'Good News.' The Information of Jesus obeying the Father, in a crucified **D**eath, **B**urial and **R**esurrection ***(DBR),*** and resurrecting with all power, according to the scriptures is simply ***AWESOME***!! By believing and receiving this Information, then applying the ***DBR*** process, ***crucified death*** and ***burial*** of unproductive words, beliefs, values, skills and habits involving people, places and things, a newness of life ***resurrects*** by the grace and rich mercies of God.

*"We are only as good as our **Information**," says Bro. Courtney Jones, Pastor, Mill Street church of Christ.*

SUCCESSFUL SELF

*(Successful Tools for Residential
Non-Governmental Transitional Housing)*

STRNGTH

This 36 Week Curriculum based on the 8 Step Eco-Map (as shown on previous page) are Successful Tools for Residential Non-Governmental Housing and is depicted as eight circles around one's core self. *(Person in Environment)* It is referred to as **STRNGTH, Phase I & Phase II** and is the spiritual component of the curriculum. The Gospel, **D**eath, **B**urial, **R**esurrection, **DBR,** is applied in 8 areas as reflected in the 8 step Eco-Map: *Spiritual, Education, Family, Career, Legal, Health (Medical/Mental), Estate (Legacy Building) and Finance.* (I Corinthians 15:1-10).

These eight (8) categories address Spirituality, Re-entry, Life Skills and Reunification for a Successful Self. A *Clinically based Person in Environment* approach is embedded also with a licensed professional counselor specializing in addictions, depression and anger management, and is the clinical component of the curriculum.

Toxic and harmful words and information affects thoughts, feelings, beliefs and behaviors, also values, skills and habits are formed by words and information. When **applying** 'Biblically' based Information, (*Word*) for a period of thirty (30) days, in each of the eight (8) areas, along with prayer and meditation, a newness of life transforms by the rich mercies and grace of God.

STRNGTH Phase I

Phase I is designated for *inmates* ages 18 and older, housed in correctional facilities (City, County, Parish, State, Federal, etc.) and desiring to participate as volunteers. The eight (8) areas identified in the 8 Step Eco Map and the *DBR* process are the successful tools that work best with a journal, purchased or provided, a Holy Bible and prayer with mediation. Each correctional facility has specific guidelines as pertaining to what is allowed, therefore adherence to their rules are encouraged.

Phase I is a 30 day self-assessment/evaluation of one's core strengths and weaknesses in each of the eight circles. This Curriculum is more helpful to a volunteer inmate if the incarcerated time is longer than a year. These self-assessments are needed to help the inner core emotional self-unveil the spirit man/woman. Practical life skills for problem-solving, based on Biblical principles are introduced and ample time, if permitted by the correctional facility, are encouraged. Greater life challenges sometimes require more time to affect permanent changes in lifestyles. Upon release from the correctional facility, transition into the *Phase II Re-entry* for aftercare is encouraged.

STRNGTH Phase II

Phase II Re-entry aftercare is an intense 36 week Curriculum based on the 8 Step Eco Map for *volunteer* former prisoners. An Intake Psychosocial and 6-month Re-assessment Psychosocial performed by a licensed, certified professional specializing in addictions, anger management and depression is required. One-on-one and small group sessions are also included in this clinical process.

Both components, spiritual and clinical, are required to be successful in the re-entry aftercare process. A Mentor, Life Skills Coach and Accountability Partner are assigned based upon individual needs. Four weekly progress notes for each of the eight areas being addressed within the 8 step Eco-Map are used to track and document the individuals' progress and success.

Referrals to other social service community programs are offered, especially financial literacy; money, economics and finance training, workforce, GED, ESL, etc. It is critical to provide appropriate information and contacts during re-entry and aftercare for an individual to be a successful self.

The Gospel Re-Enacted

**STRNGTH Phase II small group sessions for at-risk age appropriate adolescents, as pertaining to their specific needs, have shown to be successful. Non-prisoner adult volunteers desiring to address addictive, enslaving behaviors in small group sessions pertaining to their specific needs have worked well also.

Unit I: "Breath of Life"
Focus: Spiritual

Lesson Concept:
"He breathed into his nostrils the breath of life, and man became a living soul." (Gen 2:7 paraphrased, italics mine).

Adam received that breath, and Eve, as a rib in Adam, then Cain and Able born of Eve, a woman. The spirit of man is but a breath from God. We are all connected to that one breath. A living soul that shares a relationship with God and each other forms a never ending circle.

The Spiritual circle of the 8 Step Eco Map opens a door to self-assess ideas and beliefs about spirit. Information is gathered and questions as to who, when, where, why and how everything began, can receive answers.

The Life Skills Coach and Accountability Partner facilitate and encourage this process for spiritual well-being in the whole man.

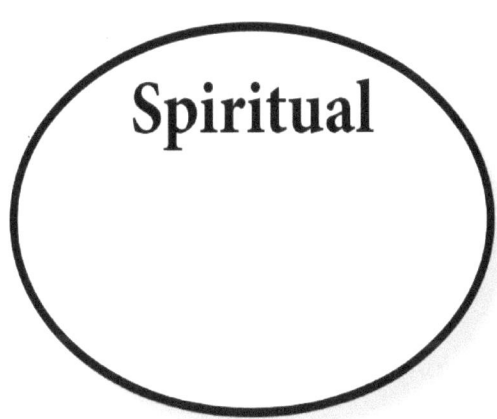

Assignment: In the circle above, write your definition or idea of what *Spiritual* means to you. On the journal page below, write or explain your ideas, beliefs and understanding about who Spirit and God are to you today. Then for the next 30 days (journal on a daily basis), with Scripture reading and word study, describe your feelings about God and your relationship with Him.

_____
_____
_____
_____
_____
_____
_____
_____
_____
_____
_____
_____
_____
_____
_____
_____
_____
_____
_____
_____
_____
_____
_____

With the Spiritual Circle in mind, use this page to draw or continue writing.

Unit II: "This is How I Learn"
Focus: Education

Lesson Concept:
God knew Jeremiah before he was formed in the womb. He sanctified and ordained him a prophet. Jeremiah was son of Hilkiah, of the priests that were in Anathoth (Jer.1:5).

This long lineage of beliefs, values, skills and habits as priests influenced Jeremiah before he entered his mother's womb. As we grow and develop, our five senses (see, smell, touch, taste hear) experience words and actions through parents, grandparents, great grandparents, friends, teachers and trusted ones. They pour knowledge into us by way of storytelling, worship, music, games, etc. And whether fathers are present or not, we are still connected to their DNA which pre-exposes us to a history of beliefs, values, skills and habits.

The Education circle of the 8 Step Eco Map helps to explore a history of life experiences by allowing a closer self- assessment and self-evaluation of our beliefs, values, skills and habits.

The Accountability Partner and Life Skills Coach will aid this exploration process using principles of **DBR** to insure that goal setting is supported by productive effective reasoning and judgment.

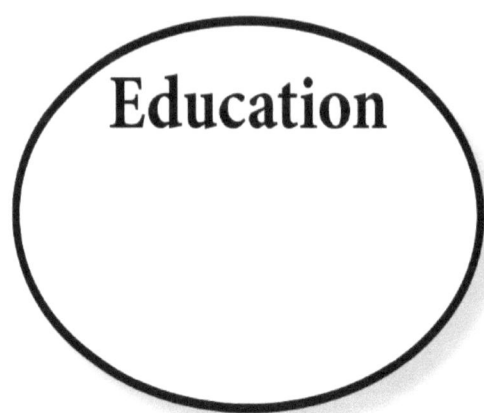

Assignment: Think about your beliefs. Where did they come from? Ask yourself, "How did I get to believe what I believe?" In the circle above, write your definition or idea of what *Education* means to you. On the journal page below, write or explain your ideas, beliefs and understanding about how you gather information. Then for the next 30 days (journal on a daily basis), with Scripture reading and word study, write about your new discoveries, experiences and feelings pertaining to your new information and new interests.

With the Education Circle in mind, use this page to draw or continue writing.

Unit III: "Where is my Father?"
Focus: Family

Lesson Concept:
GOD is a father to the fatherless and gives them fair judgment. (Ps. 68:5, 82:3 paraphrased, italics mine).

Fathers are protectors, providers, priests and prophets of the family. When fathers manage their families properly, children gain their identities and receive their lineage from their father's seed. A son learns to imitate the father, respect authority, follow rules, and establish boundaries. A daughter learns to feel loved and give it to others appropriately. Her sense of security and safety enables her to live as an organized and structured leader in her environment and her community.

The Family circle of the 8 Step Eco Map helps identify the inner conflicting thoughts and feelings that comes from having an absent father. Unfortunately there are many absent fathers in families. Research indicates most anger and depression found in young school age children and ex-offenders seem to be related to having an absent father.

This curriculum recognizes the importance of having both parents in the family.

The Life Skills Coach provides and discusses **DBR** principles that validates image, functionality, belongingness and addresses feelings of rejection, abandonment, emptiness, etc.

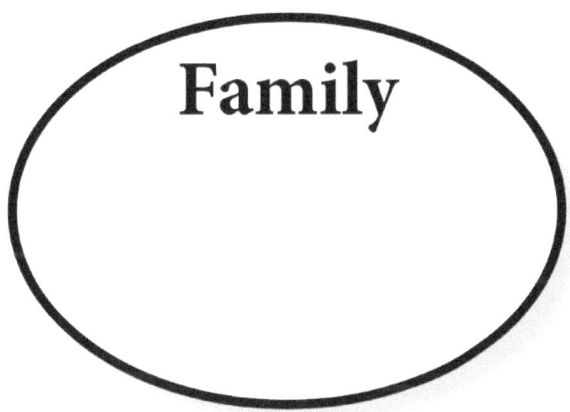

Assignment: In the circle above, write or draw your relationship with your natural father and family today. On the journal page below, write or explain the relationship you desire and would like to have with your natural father. Then for the next 30 days (journal on a daily basis), with Scripture reading and word study, describe your feelings and experiences about your journey to developing a relationship with your natural father and Father in Heaven.

___
___
___
___
___
___
___
___
___
___
___
___
___
___
___
___
___
___
___
___
___
___

With the Family Circle in mind, use this page to draw or continue writing.

Unit IV: "I was called…"
Focus: Career

Lesson Concept:
*Every good and perfect gift comes from Him, and i*t is 'Eternal.' *Be humble, gentle, patient and receive your gift(s). Walk worthy of your call to glorify Him.* (Eph. 4:1, 8, Jas. 1:17). *Jesus ascended up high and led captivity captive to give each one of us gifts, according to the measure of His grace. A man's gift makes room for him and leads him before great men.* (Pro. 18:16 paraphrased, italics mine).

According to Scripture, *a child enters the womb with gifts, from the mind of God.* (Jer. 1:5 paraphrased, italics mine). The Father gives everything needed for fruitfulness in this life, and it is all to honor Him. Receive your God given gifts and perform them on earth as you will in heaven. REJOICE!!!

These eternal gifts are easily recognized by others throughout life. They identify them in casual conversation with statements like, "Your voice is very soothing to me." "You are very artistic and expressive with your hands." Observant and wise parents recognize these gifts early on in their children, communicate them and provide proper training for the enhancement of these gifts. If schools, universities, training facilities and loved ones fail to recognize these unique gifts, then that soul may possibly experience dilemmas in successful living.

What a tragedy!!!

The Career circle of the 8 Step Eco Map explores how career, calling, vocation, gifts, etc., are introduced in youthful training. *(Pro. 22:6).*

A Mentor and Life Skills Coach helps individuals identify and recognize their 'Eternal' gifts and discuss the benefits of how they are linked to an entrepreneurial spirit that can develop into a lifetime income.

Assignment: In the circle above describe your gift(s). On the journal page below, write or explain the first time you were made aware of your God-given gift(s). Then for the next 30 days (journal on a daily basis), with Scripture reading and word study, write your feelings about your gift(s) and describe how they fit into your life, family, community and economy.

With the Career Circle in mind, use this page to draw or continue writing.

Unit V: "Eye Witness"
Focus: Legal

Lesson Concept:
*The Spirit affirms Information (**Word**) as a witness because the Spirit is truth. There are three that bear record in heaven, the Father, the Word and the Holy Ghost: and these three are one. And there are three that bear witness on earth, the Spirit and the water and the blood: and these three agree as one. If we receive the witness of men, the witness of God is greater.* (I John 5:6-9 paraphrased, italics mine).

The Legal circle of the 8 Step Eco Map challenges many beliefs, values, skills and habits that come from loved ones and are acquired during a lifetime. *But where is wisdom found? Where does understanding dwell?* (Job 28:12, paraphrase, italics mine). The first nine chapters of Proverbs are everyday practical life skills handed down by fathers to their children, especially sons, for adulthood and relationships in family, business and leadership. Just another reminder of the importance of having the presence of a father.

A Life Skills Coach and Accountability Partner aids and helps navigate the pathway of the individual's unique legal journey of rules, boundaries, principles, etc., and to provide **DBR** principles for practical daily life skills.

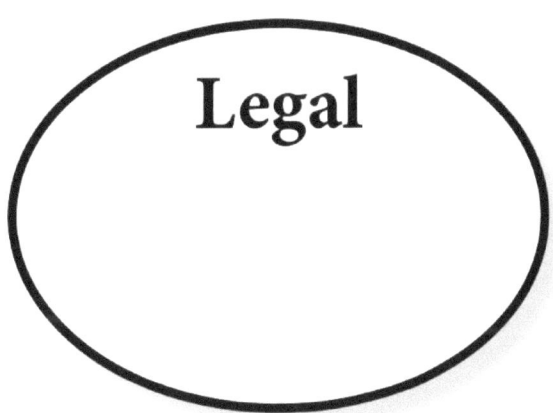

Assignment: In the circle above, define *Legal*. On the journal page below, write or explain your understanding of laws, principles, rules and boundaries. Then for the next 30 days (journal on a daily basis), with Scripture reading and word study, describe your feelings and newfound understanding and respect for the legal process of principles, rules, freedoms, etc.

With the Legal Circle in mind, use this page to draw or continue writing.

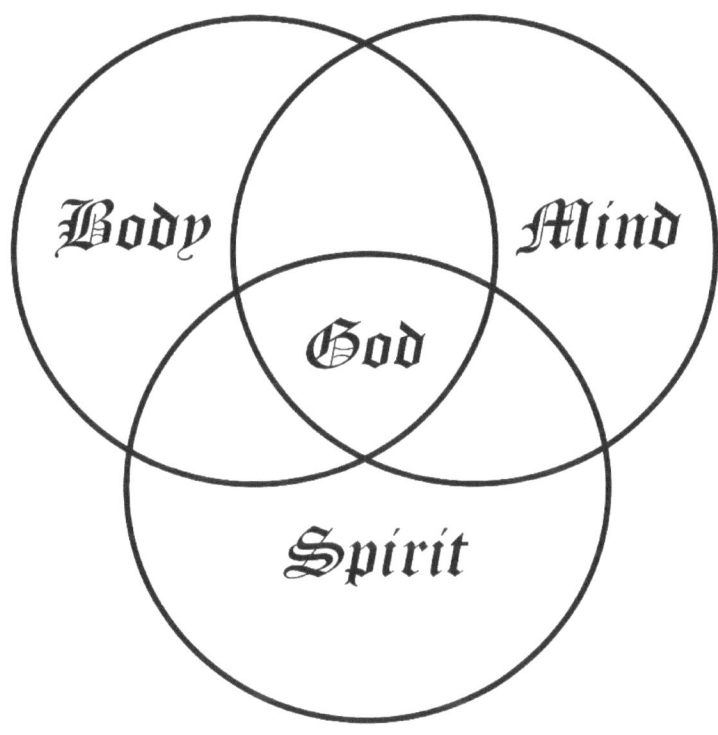

Unit VI: "Fit for the Kingdom"
Focus: Health: Medical/Mental

Lesson Concept:
My beloved friend, I pray that everything is going well for you and that your body is as healthy as your soul is prosperous. (3 John 1:1-2 paraphrased, italics mine).

There is a fearful and wonderful connection between mind, body and spirit/soul, so trust the Lord and be not wise in your own eyes or understanding. As fathers function as protectors and providers for their family, children learn how to guard their thoughts with sincere and pure imaginations. Mothers play a significant role also, by instructing them with simple and wise instructions on how to conduct themselves with sayings like; "*Play fair, always tell the truth, look up and reach high for the star, be thankful and grateful, focus on what is in front of you, not backward, speak pleasant words to others, and think before you act."* (Pro 3:8 4:22, 12:18, 13:17, 16:24 paraphrased, italics mine) These directives can help achieve a merry heart. Believe it or not, *a merry heart is like a medicine.* (Pro 17:22 paraphrased, italics mine).

The Health (Medical/Mental) circle of the 8 Step Eco Map can seem to be much more strenuous than a 30 minute cardio workout when the mind is worked-out. The mind, body and soul connection can experience peace and ease by following Biblical principles and possibly escape dis-ease and dis-harmony.

A Mentor and Life Skills coach instructs in the ***DBR*** principles for wholeness and healing.

Assignment: In the circle above, write your definition and idea of what *Health (Medical/Mental)* means to you. On the journal page below, write or explain your understanding of mind, body, spirit/soul connection. Then for the next 30 days (journal on a daily basis), with Scripture reading and word study, describe your journey of changes that brings harmony, wholeness and balance.

___

With Health (Medical/Mental) Circle in mind, use this page to draw or continue writing.

Unit VII: "A Full House"
Focus: Estate (Legacy Building)

Lesson Concept:
God made **'them'** *(male and female) after His form and function, then* ***'blessed them.'*** *"Be fruitful, multiply and populate the earth. I make you trustees of my estate, so care for 'My' creation and dominate over the fish of the sea, the birds of the sky, and every creature that roams across the earth).* (Gen 1:26-28 paraphrased, italics mine).

He blessed **'them'** *and strengthened* **'them'** *to care, dominate, lead and be productive. The estate belongs to God, and* ***He gave 'them'*** *a strong healthy body and a beautiful environment to function as good stewards, managing His estate in a responsible and accountable manner.*

The Estate circle of the 8 Step Eco-Map provides Information ***(Word)*** and instruction as to what has been made available to ***'them'*** and encourages their spirit with entrepreneurial opportunities.

A Mentor and Life Skills Coach address toxic information, ideas, beliefs, etc., that set up fears and hinder the spirit from exploring entrepreneurial opportunities with ***DBR*** principles. An Accountability Partner helps ***'them'*** make connections with community incubator programs, chambers, schools, etc. that will build and strengthen one's legacy.

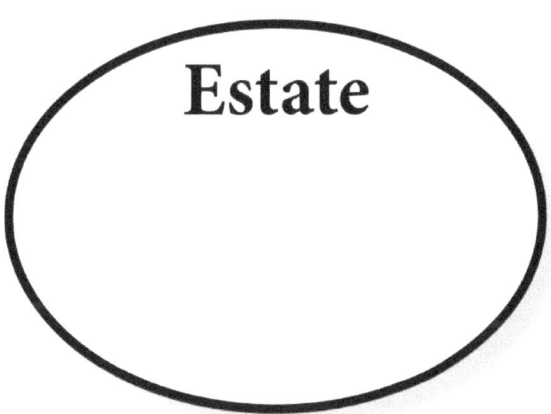

Assignment: In the circle above write your definition and idea of *Estate*. On the journal page below, write or explain your current Estate. For the next 30 days (journal on a daily basis), with Scripture reading and word study, describe your feelings, discoveries and ventures about how you function as a steward with responsibility and accountability over your gifts, talents and treasures.

With the Estate Circle in mind, use this page to draw or continue writing.

Unit VIII: "A Helpful Tool"
Focus: Finance

Lesson Concept:
*For the **<u>love</u>** of money is the root of all evil: it is through this craving that some has been led astray and have wandered from the faith and pierced themselves through with many acute [mental] pangs.* (I Tim 6:10 (AMP). ***<u>God</u>** so loved the world that He **<u>gave</u>** His only son, and God is love.* (John 3:16; I John 4:8 paraphrased, *italics mine).*

<u>Love</u> has been so misinterpreted and miscommunicated. There is a ***<u>love</u>*** *of sweets*, so they are craved. There is a ***<u>love</u>*** of things, so they are yearned for. There is a ***<u>love</u>*** of money, so it is longed for. But ***<u>love gives</u>***, and this is overlooked.

The Finance circle of the 8 Step Eco Map explores how God 'so' loved the world and shows how love is learned from God *(Genesis 2:10-15)*.

A Mentor, Life Skills Coach and Accountability Partner will function as a team in small group sessions to create a community of loving and supportive relationships built on trust. It is important for participants to experience and understand their value in community; where they fit, how they belong, and who they assist. Giving of time, talents and treasures with love to family, community and the economy is successful living.

Assignment: In the circle above, write your definition of *Finance*. On the journal pages below, write about your examples of money. For the next 30 days (journal on a daily basis), with Scripture reading and word study, describe your discoveries and experiences about the purpose of money, economics and finance. How does the tool of money relate to God, others and you?

_____
_____
_____
_____
_____
_____
_____
_____
_____
_____
_____
_____
_____
_____
_____
_____
_____
_____
_____
_____

With the Financial Circle in mind, use this page to draw or continue writing.

CELEBRATION!!

Congratulations!

You have completed the STRNGTH Phase I & Phase II - 36 Week Curriculum based on the 8 Step Eco Map. The hope is that this Information *(Word)* for re-entry and aftercare be transformational to you and others.

In the circle, write your definition or idea of **Celebration** and **Victory** and how you plan to celebrate. On the remaining journal page, write a letter to God thanking Him for newness of life, the one occurring within you and around your loved ones. Include in your letter words of love, peace, thankfulness, joy, etc. Tell Him how His love, grace and mercy filled you and how you fill others with the same. Let '*thank you*' be a permanent phrase in your everyday conversations to God, others and yourself.

Next, write a letter to your old self (the person you were before this process) and anyone else that contributed to that development. Include words of love, forgiveness, grace, mercy, peace, etc.

Lastly, write a letter to the babe (the new, resurrected *YOU!*) with a commitment to continue on this path of newness of life. Include words like; time, talents, treasures, steward, entrepreneur, responsibility, accountability, leadership, management, estate, wealth, etc.

Describe the life you dream of and make a vison board to see it. Let it reflect life more abundantly through Christ!

Thirty-six (36) weeks!   Nine (9) months!   New birth!   New you!

With the Celebration Circle in mind, use this page to draw, continue writing or start your vision board.

Conclusion

Just because you've completed this 36 Week Curriculum based on the 8 Step Eco Map does not mean you have learned all there is to know, especially about yourself. Learning is a lifetime venture, and learning about Jesus is key. Let your faith in Jesus grow to full spiritual maturity. Continue with your journal, even if you need to purchase a new one. Also, continue scripture reading and study to show yourself approved unto God, only. Practice what the Holy Spirit of God manifests to you, and tell others about this 36 Week Curriculum with the very unique 8 Step Eco Map.

Remember, growth is a lifelong process! Forget and forgive the past or you may become depressed. Avoid waiting for the future or you may become anxious! Live in the present, you are a gift!

Let us hear from you about your newness of life journey and how we can better help. Contact us via email. Visit our website and leave your comments. Like us on Facebook. Share us with your friends.

Book a Training, Seminar or Workshop.

God Bless,

Gene R. Hill, Sr. & Brenda Hill
successfulselfinc@gmail.com
http://successfulselfinc.com

Fatherhood Statistics

1. www.fatherhood/content/dad-stats

2. www.fatherhood.org/father-absence-statistics

3. https://www.fatherhood.gov/content/dad-stats

4. http://fatherhood.about.com/

5. http://www.samhsa.gov/data/sites/

6. https://fatherlessgeneration.wordpress.com/

7. http://www.cdc.gov/violenceprevention/childmaltreatment/essentials.html

8. http://differentway4kids.blogspot.com/2012/13/fatherlessness.html

9. www.cdc.gov/violenceprevention/acestudy

About the Authors

Gene R. Hill, Sr. multi-craftsman and inventor, married Brenda McArthur Blount, an Elementary Special Education Teacher in 1991. Together they blended a mixed family of 15 children (his, hers, ours and others').

Known as "Brother Hill," Gene signed up for the prison ministry in 1993 and Brenda signed up and began working with women and girls in 1995. They recognized various offending behaviors that existed in prisons, the work place, Bible classes, restaurants, public office, highways and byways, etc. They saw how these behaviors placed stumbling blocks in the paths of others and caused them to fall, distrust, or make unjust judgments about others. These offending behaviors transcended age, race, gender, etc. The term **"Offender"** took on a different meaning, and a great passion with desire stirred in the Hills to address these at risk behaviors in youth; to help circumvent their path of a possible life of incarceration, in others and in themselves.

Successful Tools for Residential Non-Governmental Transitional Housing, known as STRNGTH: A 36 Week Curriculum based on the 8 Step Eco-Map was developed. This Divine inspiration comprises twenty five (25) years of life experiences with diverse personalities and challenges in blended families, various ministries, and community lobbying for the at risk, incarcerated and the former prison population.

Successful Self, Inc. is a 501c3 non-profit corporation formed in Jan. 2009.
Find out more by visiting http://successfulselfinc.com

www.ingramcontent.com/pod-product-compliance
Lightning Source LLC
Chambersburg PA
CBHW061400090426
42743CB00002B/85